History Makers
Your mission from God

Andy and Catherine Kennedy

Authentic LIFESTYLE

SPRING HARVEST
Equipping the Church for action

First published 2003 by Spring Harvest Publishing Division and Authentic Lifestyle.

09 08 07 06 05 04 03   7 6 5 4 3 2 1
Authentic Lifestyle is a division of Authentic Media,
9 Holdom Avenue, Bletchley, Milton Keynes, Bucks, MK1 1QR, UK.

British Library Cataloguing in Publication Data
A catalogue record for this book is available from the British Library

1-85078-514-7

Cover and text design by Giles Davies Design
Illustrations by Giles Davies
Printed in Great Britain by Bell and Bain Ltd, Glasgow

CONTENTS

Check This Out Kids!

What is 'The Big Cell'?

It's ten weeks of material designed especially for children aged 8–12, to help them lead their own cells.

What is a Cell?

A cell is a small group of about 3–7 children, who get together to pray for their friends and the world, have fun, explore the Bible, listen to God and get to know Him better. Jesus said that 'if two or three people come together in my name, I am there with them.' (Matthew 18:20)

Wow! So cell is a place where you can expect to meet Jesus.

Here are five important things a cell should aim for:

1   Jesus at the centre
2   Care and Belonging
3   Everyone with a part to play
4   Servant leadership
5   Prayer

How Do Cell Sessions Work?

They work using Four Ws:

Welcome   – time for fun together
Worship   – time to focus on God and tell Him how great He is
Word   – time to explore the Bible
Work it Out – time to pray and get practical.

You will see these 'Four Ws' as you read through this book. We recommend you share out the Ws so a different member of the cell leads each one. You could change the leaders every week!

We also suggest a fifth W – **a Wise Person** – an adult who helps the cell. They might be in the room with you when you meet, they might be in the next room or nearby. If you decide to start a cell, you need to decide as a group who your Wise Person is going to be. They might be one of your parents, a children's leader in your church, or some one else who knows Jesus well. Ask this person to pray about being your adult supporter who you can go to with questions, problems, prayer needs and so on.

How Long Does a Cell Session Last?

Every session is designed to last an hour. Each W has the number of minutes it should take written underneath. The sessions could of course last longer or shorter depending on how much you pray, talk etc!

Getting Started...

When will you meet? Talk to your friends, put some dates in your diaries. We suggest you find a time and stick to it each week. It could be at school during lunchtime, after school in one of your homes or a Sunday afternoon. We already know of one cell where they meet for breakfast each Sunday. Make sure you all check out the time you choose with your family – they may have things planned!

What Cell is Not...

Cell is not a replacement for what you do at church with your leaders. You need to pray for your leaders and find ways to encourage them through what you do in cell.

It is not a gang that makes other people feel left out. You need to be careful about this right from the beginning, and get advice from your Wise Person if you think there may be a chance of this.

Check This Out Grown Ups!

What is 'The Big Cell'?

'The Big Cell' is material specifically designed for children aged 8–12 to use in peer-led cells, with the help and advice of a wise adult.

Peer-led Children's Cells?

Isn't That a Bit Dangerous?

The Big Cell recognises that leadership ability is evident in young people even before they hit adolescence and their teen years. Many children in our churches are so well fed that they are 'fed up'. Few, however, are really given the chance to exercise the gifts God has given them, to take a lead and to rely on God in new ways. Cells are one way in which children can take on leadership and responsibility in 'bite-sized chunks' with the covering and support of their 'Wise Person'.

Does this fit my situation?

You may have a group of children who you know are ready for this challenge. You may have a group who still need an adult's supervision, but are ready to be given a chance to lead. You may just be looking for new material to use with your children's group! There is no reason why this material could not be used in any of these circumstances, whether led by children or adults.

Who is the 'Wise Person'?

The structure of each session is based on four Ws – 'Welcome', 'Worship', 'Word' and 'Work it Out'. These aspects are explained further in the *Check This Out Kids!* page.

We have added a fifth W – the 'Wise Person'. This is the mature adult who fulfils an important role in the cell through supporting and guiding the children without taking control in any way. They would not necessarily need to be present during cell sessions – in fact, this might inhibit some children! A Wise Person may be in the next room or a phone call away. Their role is to help the children prepare, to answer questions, to provide debrief after sessions and to help sort out any problems arising. Above all, they should lovingly and prayerfully encourage the children in their quest to know God better.

One idea to consider is to organise a short meeting of all parents and children to share the vision and values of 'The Big Cell'. It would be an excellent start for the children to have their parents pray for them.

The Big Cell Web Site:

www.kingskidsengland.co.uk

You may be interested to know that there is a Web site where children's cells can connect with each other, find out what God is doing among them across the nation and get fresh ideas and inspiration. Children must make sure they do this with their parent's knowledge and agreement. Why not log in together as a whole cell along with the Wise Person?

'The Big Cell' is a ministry of King's Kids England. King's Kids is a part of Youth With A Mission.

Things To Help Your Cell Times

Be Prepared!

This material is laid out so that you as a cell group can divide the responsibilities up for the session. If you agree to lead one of the W sections for a cell group do not turn up at cell group expecting it all to just happen.

It is very important to be prepared in advance. This material will only work if you get your props and equipment ahead of time.

For most sessions you will need the following:
A Bible (we use the International Children's Bible – New Century Version)
A CD/cassette player, plus CDs/cassettes as suggested in the session
Paper and pens
The Worship Wall

> **YOU WILL NEED**
> lots of newspaper
> a long piece of rope

In addition, the 'You will need' panel will tell you what extra things you need to get hold of before the session.

Treat your part seriously and pray about it. Do it for God first and foremost. If you have problems in your preparation, then give another member of the cell a call, or call the Wise Person.

● ●

The Worship Wall

A Worship Wall is a great thing to have for your cell group worship time. You could make one very easily with some card and paint, and use it in all sorts of ways. It could be a place to:

● Stick prayers of thanks and praise to God
● Bring things you want to offer back to God
● Stick worship poems
● Place models and pictures you have created in worship

Your group will probably think of loads more ideas!

See Appendix A for more instructions, and signs to photocopy.

The Journal

A Journal is like a diary that you can write in every week as part of Cell. The 'Work it Out' section often has an activity for you to do in your Journal.

It's great to be able to look back and see what you were thinking about and praying for, especially when you see God answering your prayers.

You can use all sorts of things as a Journal:

- A Notebook
- A Diary
- A Scrapbook
- Lots of pieces of paper stapled together!

Why not cover your Journal with funky paper, and put your cell group's name on it (as well as your own). You could design a logo on the computer. Why not meet as a group and all have fun doing it together!

You will know it's time to use your Journal when you see the words:

Remember to bring your Journal to cell group every time you meet.

1 History Makers know His-story

welcome

You can either do both of the activities below or choose just one. If you do both, be careful to keep to the time given.

Group story

Ask for a volunteer to start up a story with the line 'Once upon a time...' then the next person in the circle continues with their sentence. Keep going round the circle adding more sentences. Use your imagination!

7 minutes

Fast runners

Find a place to run this relay race safely. It could be your garden path or the pavement by your home.

▶ Divide into two teams if there are enough of you.

▶ Take it in turns to run and pass each other the baton, just like in a relay race. Record your times.

▶ In a few weeks, you might want to try again and improve on your team performance.

5 minutes

YOU WILL NEED

two cardboard insides of kitchen towel rolls or something similar

YOU WILL NEED

strong thick cardboard

sponges and poster paint

'History Maker' by Martin Smith

YOU WILL NEED

a cut up copy of the first 3 pages of appendix B

Hand print and sing

▶ Today the cell group will make the Worship Wall. This will be used for the next ten weeks, so make it good and strong. (See instructions in Appendix A.)

▶ Sing the song 'History Maker' by Martin Smith once through, then again as you paint hand marks onto the Worship Wall.

▶ Then pray. What do you want to say to God? 'Here I am ready for you to use.' 'Lord, I surrender my life to you.' Or 'Lord, I give myself, and the gifts, abilities and talents you have given me, back to you.'

10 minutes

Sorting out His-story

There is a sorting activity to complete as a group. You will find it in Appendix B (page 53).

10 minutes

World mission quiz

(Answers are in Appendix D (page 58). Please don't spoil it by cheating!)

★ Approximately how many nations are there in the world?

  a 107   **b** 230   **c** 389

★ What is the population of the world as at the beginning of 2003?

  a 100 million   **b** 4.6 billion   **c** 6.2 billion

★ How many of the world's 13,000 different people groups still don't have any of the Bible in their own language?

  a more than 1,000 **b** more than 3,000 **c** more than 6,000

★ Which is the second most followed faith after Christianity?

  a Hinduism   **b** Buddhism   **c** Islam

★ How any people are estimated to have seen the *Jesus* film in the world?

  a 50 million   **b** 3.5 billion   **c** 4.1 billion

★ If there was only one Christian in the world and he/she led someone to Jesus in the first year and then in the second year they both led another person each, how long before the whole world is full of Christians?

  a 34 years   **b** 10 years   **c** 100 years

5 minutes

Sergio from Bolivia

My name is Sergio. I'm 8 years old and I live in Santa Cruz in Bolivia. My Mum became a Christian a few years ago and started taking me to church with her. Now I love God too and I want to serve Him.

One day when we were coming home from church, we were walking past lots of houses. I asked Mum who lived in them, but she didn't know. I asked her if they loved Jesus like we do, but she said that they probably didn't.

Next Sunday I went to talk to the Pastor. I asked him if we could go to the people's houses and tell them about Jesus, but he said he'd have to think about it. The next Sunday I went to talk to him again, but he said he hadn't thought about it yet. The third Sunday he said that he'd thought about it and didn't think it was a very good idea.

All those three weeks, I'd been thinking about it too and I'd been praying for the people when we walked past their houses. I thought about how sad it was that they didn't know God. I thought about how sad God must be that they weren't His friends. I decided that even if no-one else would tell them about God, I would. Then I heard about a King's Kids outreach coming to my city. I asked if I could be a part of it. I'm so glad that I'm finally getting to let people know about Jesus and how much He loves them.

I also pray a lot for Japan. There are lots of people there who don't know God either. I've started taking Japanese classes in the Japanese Centre in my city. It's a bit difficult to learn, but God is helping me. As soon as I can I want to go to Japan and tell the people there about God's love for them.

BOLIVIA

4 minutes

We are the final chapter

See what Jesus asks you to do in Matthew 28:16–20
People call it 'The Great Commission'. It's worth memorising.
Are you willing to become a History Maker?

Journal Time

 What dreams and visions do you have to extend the Kingdom of God?
Write them in your journal.

★ Key Idea

Which runners are put in the last places of the relay team? Yes, the fastest! That's you guys then. God has put you in at the end of the race; at the end of His-story. Don't wait for the starter's pistol. The race has already begun. Now, get ready and take the baton as it's passed to you. 'On your marks, get set, go!'

That's what the next nine cell sessions are about – connecting into the mission of God and discovering your part in it all, your destiny. It's not just about the next few weeks of cell but for the rest of your life!

Creative prayer idea

Prayer cube

Make the prayer cube in Appendix C.
Each person takes a turn to roll the cube and then everyone prays for what it suggests. Take two minutes for each prayer.

18 minutes

Useful Resource to ask your Wise Person about

Have you or anyone else in the church got the missions prayer book called *Operation World* (see Useful resources section)? It has some Web site and email addresses, of mission groups that can help you more.

Please check with your Wise Person before going on the internet. Perhaps they would like to have a look at the site with you. Why not try Mission Aviation Fellowship first and see if they have stuff for kids.

www.maf.org

2 History Makers need power

Do both of the suggested activities, but please keep to the times given.

Arm wrestling

Get into pairs and have an arm wrestling tournament – the winners of each pair play each other until you have your winner. Make sure you have a table to rest your elbows on. Alternatively, you could lie down on the carpet. If you are at a table the rule is 'elbows are not allowed to be lifted up!' You may need to appoint a good referee!

5 minutes

YOU WILL NEED
table or carpet

Power lungs

- Give each person two plates.

- One plate should have 10 sweets on and the other should be empty.

- Make sure that everyone's plates are the same distance apart.

- See who can suck up the 10 sweets with the straw and transfer them from one plate to the other the fastest.

- No hands allowed to pick up the sweets!

5 minutes

YOU WILL NEED
2 plates, 1 straw,
10 maltesers
(or similar sweet)
per person

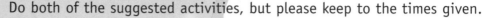

Top tunes

The leader of this section needs to ask three people in the cell to come prepared for sharing one song each that they like, each person saying why they have chosen it.

- Play each song and worship God together.

- At the Worship Wall put up the word 'Power' to remind you of today's theme.

10 minutes

More good news

Last week we talked about the job Jesus has for us – to become History Makers in God's story. The good news is that we don't have to do this on our own. God's amazing idea was for Him to help us by living inside each one of us who believe. Wow!

Read Joel 2:28–29

When Joel wrote this down it was way before Jesus was born. Here the Holy Spirit is prophesied and promised to be given to everyone who is a servant and friend of God.

Prophecy comes true

Read Acts 1:8 and Acts 2:1–4,17 to see when Joel's prophecy began to come true. Big Peter the fisherman and disciple of Jesus even said it!

Splash factor

What is the power in us? It is God, the Holy Spirit.

Pour the water into the glass and watch the water splash out. If you pour it from a greater height there is a greater force and it splashes out even more. The secret of mission and evangelism is the power of God so filling us that He splashes out from our lives to those around us; they can't help but see something different in us. They may even ask us what it is we have.

15 minutes

'God didn't send the Comforter to make us comfortable, but rather to make us missionaries!' (Michael Green)

Did you know?

What is a 'missionary'? Well, the word means 'a sent one'.
You will not find the word 'missionary' in the Bible, but the idea is everywhere in it. The usual word used by the translators is the word 'apostle'. It is the same idea and means one who is sent out like an ambassador going on a mission.

YOU WILL NEED

jug of water

a glass and a basin to catch the overflow

Robert is 13 and from a housing scheme in Glasgow, Scotland. Listen to his story of being 'sent'.

Robert was on his first mission trip to England and he was very excited. During the week he spent there he visited several towns in the Midlands. The children and young people would gather at the beginning of each day to pray and ask God what He wanted to do that day. Robert saw in his mind a picture of a boy sitting on a bench in the town centre where he was to go that afternoon. This boy was wearing a red top, had a mobile phone and was wearing blue tracksuit bottoms. Robert told us all about this 'picture' and we all began to pray for him. Later that afternoon as the team were out in Hinckley, Robert saw the boy – just as he had pictured in his mind! Robert and his friends went over to him and told him that Jesus loved him and that they had been praying for him.

It is good to know that God speaks to us today and it really encouraged Robert too!

2 minutes

SCOTLAND

Glasgow

Vinegar and chips

When we read 'filled' in the New Testament it means being 'soaked' or 'drenched with', as with water. It would be the same word if we talked of putting vinegar all over our chips!

Creative prayer idea

Soak it up!

Pass the basin and sponge around the group. Each person soaks the sponge in the water and squeezes it back out a few times. As they do so someone else in the group prays for the Holy Spirit to fill that person just like the sponge soaks up the water! Pray for them to be filled with power. When you get prayed for, your job is to agree and thank God for filling you afresh.

10 minutes

Did you know?

We are given a command in the Bible to be filled with the Holy Spirit. You can read this in Ephesians 5:18. Actually, the original Greek language the Bible was written in says 'Go on being filled with the Holy Spirit'.

Prayer cube

Have another few minutes with the cube you made last week. Focus the praying on Scotland this time.

6 minutes

Web sites to check out

Please make sure you ask your parents or Wise Person before you go on-line. Tell your Wise Person about what you have learnt from these sites.

New Tribes Mission **www.ntm.org**

TEAM **www.teamworld.org**

WEC International **www.wec-int.org**

3 History Makers need God's heart for people

Hide 'n' seek

Choose one person to be the 'seeker'. The others must hide themselves around the room, house or garden. They have 60 seconds to hide. The seeker only has 3 minutes to find everyone. If the seeker manages to do this then they receive a prize, if not then the 'hiders' get a prize! Now give someone else a turn.

10 minutes

Pure hearts

► Read Psalm 24:3–4

► As you start worship today, put on a quiet worship song (e.g. 'Open the eyes of my heart Lord'), and take a minute to quietly ask the Holy Spirit to show you anything you need to say sorry to Him for. Make sure also that you are right with each other.

► Put the words 'God's Heart' onto the Worship Wall.

► Write down the things you feel God is saying onto your heart shape, and then each say a prayer out loud to say you are sorry.

► When you have all finished, take them all to the toilet and flush them away. This shows exactly what God does when he forgives you and makes your heart clean.

10 minutes

Father God cares for lost and hurting people

This can be hard for us to do by ourselves; we can all be very selfish. The only way we are going to be able to do this is with help! Whose? Yes...God the Holy Spirit again comes to the rescue! His job is to help us become more like Him. He can help us grow special qualities inside us called kindness and goodness (see the fruit of Holy Spirit in Galatians 2:22–23).

Lost sheep story

Most of us have heard Jesus' well-known story about the hundred sheep and the one that got lost. Read it together.

Matthew 18:12–14

TO THINK ABOUT

God isn't willing for one person or child to get lost. But are you? Am I? Is the church? Do we care at all?

Sheep and goats

Here is a challenging bit of the Bible to read. Watch out!

Read Matthew 25:31–40

Discuss

▶ What sort of people is Jesus concerned that we look after?

▶ What special word does Jesus call them by (v.40)?

▶ What does this tell us about how He sees them?

15 minutes

Lena is a 9-year-old Egyptian girl

Last week we went to visit an orphanage for girls. My leaders asked me to pray and to arrange a Christmas gift for a girl of 5. Her name is Mary. I was very happy and arranged a box full of toys and stuff. I was told it must be new stuff or at least in very good condition. I started to pray for Mary and I felt I needed to give up one of my new Christmas gifts, given this year, and some books which will show Mary how much God loves her.

On the day we went to the orphanage I was really looking forward to the visit, and when I got there it was clean, but very small for all those girls. I started to look for Mary (it was my first time to see her). I found her, a small skinny girl with scratch on her face. I was in trouble. I forgot all the words in my mind, but I started with giving her the little gift and I said to her 'God loves you'. She smiled a very big smile and quickly started to open her gift. I stayed and played with her for about an hour and I told her the story in the book. After that we all prayed together before we left the orphanage. I left Mary with the same big smile on her face.

Cairo
EGYPT

Emilse is 12 years old and comes from Argentina

I am 12 years old, but I have 8 brothers and sisters who are younger than me. Mum is often ill when she's pregnant and it's difficult for her to look after us all, but she tries. My job is to find enough food for us to eat and get all the things we need. I work most of the day at the rubbish dump trying to find useful things to sell. Sometimes I do washing for people, but in winter the water is very cold and the skin on my hands breaks and they start to bleed. When they hurt a lot, I just think of my mum and brothers and sisters at home. I love them so much. I don't really know my dad, but God has been a good father to me. I think if it wasn't for him helping me, I would always be worrying about getting enough for everyone, but I know that He's the one who is looking after us. He's with me all day and He looks after me. He helps me to look after the others too.

ARGENTINA

4 Minutes

Who wants to do something for Jesus?

Compare Matthew 25:40 with Matthew 18:5.

Did you realise that when you help someone in need or even a little child, then Jesus is touched too?

Journal Time

► Who do you know? You might not know people in prison or as poor as Jesus talked about but you might know someone who Jesus would call the 'least of these brothers of mine'.

► Do you know someone who gets left out, called a loser, picked on, or who is not looked after properly, at your school?

► Write down their names and what their problem is in your journal.

Creative prayer idea

Be quiet!

Pray now as a cell for these people. Ask God to show you how much He loves them. Ask God for help in loving them too. Be silent for one minute, asking God how, practically, you could care for them. Write down what you are going to do this week about it as an individual or a cell.

Prayer cube

Take turns to roll the cube again and this time focus your prayers on Egypt and Paraguay. Make sure you have your world map or globe handy so you know where these countries are.

20 minutes

Web sites to check out

Remember to ask permission first, or log on with your Wise Person and check them out together.

Tearfund **www.tearfund.org/youth**

OMF International **www.omf.org.uk**

Church Mission Society **www.cms-uk.org**

YOU WILL NEED

journals and pens
prayer cube
world map/globe

4 History Makers know that prayer works

Chopsticks race

Each person gets a pair of chopsticks. Practise for a minute using them. Each person gets 2 small plates. One is empty and the other is full of Jelly Babies. See who can pick up and transfer the most from one plate to the empty one in the time you agree. No stabbing the Jelly Babies! Try and use the sticks properly! We suggest 3–4 minutes is long enough. At the end of the game you can all enjoy eating the Jelly Babies.

8 minutes

YOU WILL NEED

a pair of chopsticks for each person

2 small plates each

large bag of Jelly Babies

Look into the future

Peep into the ultimate worship experience ever, and guess what, you are there if you love and follow Jesus! As you are reading about it, look out for the two body postures or positions mentioned.

Read Revelation 7:9–17

Did you notice? Yes, that's right – standing up and lying down!

Change position

Choose a couple of songs. One suggestion would be from Tim Hughes' CD *Here I am to worship* (2001 Survivor Records) As you all use the songs to worship, change your body position. Bow down, or kneel, or lie flat out, or stand with hands outstretched. The Bible says 'bring a sacrifice of praise'. That means something that costs you to do it! Someone put up the words 'Prayer Works' on the Worship Wall.

10 minutes

More workers needed. Pray!

Ask a couple of people to read this out loud.

Luke 10:1–12

Jesus realised that one of the main challenges to getting the job done would be not having enough workers to do it. The harvest field would be ripe and ready, but the farmer would be desperate for staff.

This is one of the times when Jesus tells us what to pray for. It's really clear! Then he tells his friends to help answer their own prayer. 'Go!', he says to them and they obey, going out in twos.

▶ What is prayer? Discuss for a few moments. What other words can help us describe it?

▶ What is intercession? Have you heard this word? It means to 'stand in the gap' or to speak to God on behalf of someone else.

Someone has said that prayer is 'creating with God'. So we are helping change history when we pray. If Jesus tells us to pray then it must really work.

12 minutes

story time

Sarah is a children's leader who works in a country where Christians are regularly arrested and hurt because they talk about Jesus – China.

I had come to teach the children about worship and prayer. It was a cold Chinese winter's night, freezing cold. It was late and I was aching and exhausted from the day's journey. Eventually I fell asleep, but then was wakened by someone shaking me. 'Teacher, teacher, wake up! Someone is here to see you.'
My mind was foggy and it took me a few minutes to realize where I was. 'What? Who? It must be past midnight! What do you need?'
'Quick. Someone is outside. They want to see you.'
'Oh, no', I thought. 'It's freezing outside. It's freezing inside! Please don't ask me to go out.' I put my icy clothes on, and stepped outside. It was pitch black. Snow was falling softly. My eyes gradually adjusted to the dark. I could make out two small figures standing rigid by the well.
'We came to see you', said one. 'We heard you have Bibles.'
'Why, yes, I do. But who sent you? Where are you from?'
'Our parents heard you would be here. They asked us to come and get Bibles. We walked, mostly at night. We had to be very careful. Our parents said it was dangerous. If anyone caught

us...well, they prayed no one would.'

'It's freezing! You've been walking alone at night by yourselves?'

'We've been walking for three months.'

I froze. Not from the cold this time, but from the reality of what they had just said. 'Three MONTHS?'

'The Holy Spirit told our parents about three months ago there would be a woman with Bibles here. It is too dangerous for them to come, but they would not notice us children.'

Suddenly I felt my cheeks grow hot. I started to cry.

'We are so thankful to finally get here. May we please have some Bibles?'

I tried to gain my composure. 'Why, yes. Of course you may have all I have left.' I quickly went to my backpack and took out the few remaining Bibles I had. I handed them to the taller of the two. As she took the Bibles, I could see the proud, joyful smile on her face. 'Thank you,' she said, and turned away.

'Wait! Where are you going?'

'Oh, we have to go back. Our parents are waiting.'

'What? You've come all this way, only to turn around and go back?'

'We have what we came for.'

'But at least stay and drink some tea. Let me give you something to eat.'

'No, we must be on our way. The whole village has been waiting for us.'

Before I could protest, they were out of my sight. Out into the freezing dark night.

CHINA

story time

Incredible prayer story

24-7 Prayer started by accident back in 1999, with a bunch of young people in England who got the crazy idea of trying to pray non-stop for a month. That was September, and when God turned up they didn't stop until Christmas!

24-7 has since then become a worldwide, non-stop prayer movement. It all links through the Web site www.24-7prayer.com. Why not visit the site as a cell and see for yourselves what God is doing.

6 minutes

Prayer cube

Roll the cube and pray for the church in China.

10 minutes

Creative prayer idea

World map

Inflatable globe – Throw the globe around from person to person, while music plays. When the music stops (someone needs to stop it), whoever is holding the globe looks under their right thumb to see which country they are touching.

Paper map – Take it in turns to be blindfolded. As the music plays, move your finger over the surface of the map and when the music stops see which country you are touching. The group should then pray for that country.

▶ Simple blessing prayers are powerful. 'God bless the nation of . . .'

▶ Ask God to send Christians there to tell the Good News.

▶ Ask God for Christians to be sent out from that nation as missionaries.

▶ Start the music again and carry on.

10 minutes

Learn more about China, Asia and 24-7

Check out these Web sites with your Wise Person

Chinese Church Support Ministries UK **www.am-ccsm.org**

Back to Jerusalem Movement (in the Chinese Church)

www.backtojerusalem.com

Asia Harvest **www.asiaharvest.org**

Road Through China **www.rtcinfo.org**

24-7 Prayer **www.24-7prayer.com**

5 History Makers are willing to hear from God

welcome

Try both of these ideas today in the Welcome time.

Whose shoes?

Someone is chosen to leave the room. Everyone else takes off their shoes and puts them in the centre of the room. The first person re-enters the room and has to decide whose shoes are whose.

5 minutes

YOU WILL NEED

sheets of newspaper

Newspaper stand problem

Play this game in pairs.

▶ Each pair is given a sheet of newspaper and told that they are not allowed to cut it up, rip it or tear it in any way.

▶ They must find a way of standing upright on the same piece of paper, facing each other, yet not be able to touch each other with any part of their bodies.

▶ If no-one has worked out the answer after about 4 minutes, give them a clue that they will probably all have to move to a different part of the room to solve the problem.

The answer is in Appendix D (page 58), ... but no cheating!

5 minutes

YOU WILL NEED

paper and scissors

Shoes off!

Someone read this out loud.

Exodus 3:1–5

When God met Moses for the first time he told him to take off his shoes. Why? It was a sign of respect and humility.

▶ What did God call the ground Moses was standing on?

▶ What does the word 'Holy' mean?

▶ Take off your shoes as a sign of respect for God.

▶ Sing a song together.

Shoes on!

Someone else read this

Ephesians 6:15

What are the shoes called? Notice how important these shoes are: they form part of the armour that God commands each believer to wear at all times. Being ready to 'Go' as Jesus leads us is vital.

▶ Cut out a shape of a pair of shoes on paper.

▶ Write on it a prayer that starts 'Here I am Lord ready and willing to....'

▶ Stick it on the Worship Wall.

10 minutes

Learn from Phil

Phil is one of only two people in the Bible called an 'evangelist'. Look this up and find out how he gets to be one.

Acts 8:1–8

It's a dangerous time, but God's people keep spreading the good news. Look what happens when Phil speaks to the crowds. Wouldn't it be amazing to see our cities filled with joy like that?

Not many of us get to preach to masses of people, although some of you may do in the future.

But look what happens now. Read verses 26–40.

God speaks to Phil through a messenger angel (v. 26). God isn't just interested in big crowds. No, he has seen a man sitting alone in a chariot travelling through the desert and this man is really hungry to know the truth and what life is all about. He's just been at a religious festival in Jerusalem but he hasn't found the answers he needs.

God decides to set up a divine appointment to rescue this man. He needs a willing volunteer. Phil says 'Yes!'

So Phil runs to catch a chariot just to get the chance to speak to one person.

The man turns out to be a very important and influential man returning to Africa. Historians believe that the start of the church in Ethiopia may have happened through this man in his chariot. Wow! What if Phil hadn't done his bit?

What do you think happened to Phil in verse 39? Was it supernatural angel transportation?

10 minutes

NORTHERN IRELAND
Belfast

storytime

There is another Phil who lives in Belfast. In 2001, he was 12 years old. That summer he felt God told him to join a King's Kids outreach and so he went to Manchester on a circus evangelism team. Out of 10,000 young Christians in Manchester that summer he was one of the youngest!

I remember Phil came to me a bit nervously one morning saying he felt God was asking him to pray publicly from the microphone when we went onto the street that afternoon to do some performances. Well, he did! He looked like a caged lion pacing up and down, radio mike in hand, asking the people of Manchester to stop and be prayed for. His raspy Belfast accent, a bit hoarse from too much shouting and praising, filled the street as he prayed. People were listening – they'd never seen anyone pray like this before! After a fairly short time, he stopped and said to everyone that it would be better if the team came and prayed personally with people. I expected the street to clear fast. It didn't. Phil handed me the mike and, without hesitation teamed up with his ministry partner and approached a man over to our left. This man in his late forties was, minutes later, accepting Jesus into his life. Amazing!

What if Phil hadn't obeyed the voice of God that day and overcome his nerves?

2 minutes

Discuss

- Has God ever given you a divine appointment where he asked you to share your faith with a friend or someone you didn't know? What happened?

- What sort of things might stop you from listening to God and obeying him?

- Does anyone in the cell feel that God may be calling them to be an evangelist?

- If anyone does, put that person in the middle of the circle and pray for God's Holy Spirit to come and empower them.

Prayer cube

Roll the dice and remember to pray for that much-troubled, but beautiful country called Northern Ireland.

7 minutes

Cell group challenge this week

Not everyone is called to be an evangelist but we are certainly all called to evangelise, to be ready to share why we love Jesus.

Here's a dangerous prayer to pray. Cut it out and use it each morning:

> Lord, if you want me to share your love and good news to someone today, I am ready and available. Just make it very clear when the time comes that it is you leading me. And Lord, when the opportunity comes, help me to be brave and seize the moment.

Next week, be ready to share any answers you get to this prayer. Keep notes in your journal.

Web site to check out with your Wise Person

YWAM and King's Kids are missions that have great stories of people who have heard God speak.

www.kingskidsengland.co.uk

www.ywam.org.uk

6 History Makers need boldness

Frantic

Split your cell into two teams. Lay the rope on the floor to divide the room in half. Each team stands in their own half with roughly equal amounts of newspaper. You have one minute to throw as much newspaper as you can into each other's halves. No one can cross or reach over the line. The winning team has the least pieces of paper when one minute is called! Have a frantic time!

5 minutes

YOU WILL NEED

lots of newspaper

a long piece of rope

YOU WILL NEED

a big sheet of paper (possibly wallpaper)

colourful felt pens

You're amazing!

▶ Put the paper on the floor so that everyone can sit around it. Think of some of the most descriptive, thought-provoking words you can about God. Not just 'good' or 'powerful' but 'MAJESTIC', 'INCREDIBLE' or 'EARTH-SHAKING'!

▶ Work together to cover the paper with your words.

▶ Now it's time to be bold. Stand around the paper and shout out, one after the other, 'God, you are...!' using some of your favourite words. Remember, this is worship – you are shouting out to God, not each other.

▶ Put the word 'Boldness' up on the Worship Wall.

10 minutes

Stephen's boldness

A few weeks ago, we looked at the time when the disciples received the Holy Spirit. Afterwards they were not afraid of what would happen to them any more – they were filled with boldness.

What were some of the bold things they began to do? (Acts 5:12–16) Stephen's story starts soon after. Read it together now.

Acts 6:8–15

Stephen was a man who was full of wisdom and God's love, but the people who kept the Jewish law could not stand him. They captured him and argued with him. He answered them boldly and explained why he did what he did. Listen to this bit – Acts 7:51–53.

They got really angry then, but Stephen still wasn't afraid. Acts 7:54–60 Wow! He even died forgiving those people, not afraid of them or death.

10 minutes

Here are two stories from children who boldly stood up for God.

story time

Salome, almost 11, is from Togo in West Africa.

A few weeks ago, one of my friends at school (Afi) had let her ruler (long and heavy) fall on an other girl's foot (Pépé). It was an accident. In revenge, Pépé told everyone in the class not to talk or play with Afi anymore. I saw what happened and didn't agree with her, so I stood up and said to the class: 'I love Jesus and because of that, I don't want to reject Afi. It was an accident and you can do what you want, but I will continue to play with her.'

I also went to Pépé and talked to her: 'God's children don't react this way. You should forgive Afi. She didn't mean to hurt you.'

A little later, Pépé went to Afi and they got reconciled. Peace came back in the class...

It's not easy to witness at school, but I'm so happy I dared to say what I believed that day.

TOGO

Elishava, age 10, is from Calgary in Canada.

I stood there tense, waiting for our music to start. I had been nervous about this moment ever since we arrived in downtown Juarez, Mexico. At the park where we were presenting, there were many gang members hanging out. My sisters and I were doing a baton dance to a Spanish song, sung by Jaci Velasquez. Just then, the music started. I waited for a second, then slowly began the moves. Just as the words to the song, 'God So Loved the World' (in Spanish, of course) began, all other activity in the park stopped and all eyes focused on my sisters and me. People were crowding closer. I was confused. This hadn't happened during other skits and dances. It made no sense. Had they never seen a baton? After everything was being packed up, almost everyone in the park became a Christian. I was very surprised to see how God used three little girls twirling batons to bring even the toughest gangsters to the Lord.

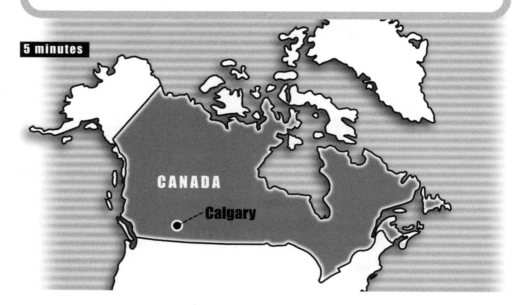

`5 minutes`

CANADA

Calgary

work it out

Discuss

- When was the last time you were asked at school or at play about your faith?

- Do people at school know you are a believer?

- Are you afraid to witness?

`5 minutes`

Role play

Choose members of the cell to play a Christian, an observer and the rest are to be their friends or fellow class students at school.

- ▶ The non-Christian friends ask the Christian questions about what and why they believe.

- ▶ Play this scenario for a few minutes and then stop and discuss how the Christian got on.

- ▶ If you like, ask someone else to play the Christian and do it again.

10 minutes

> If you were on trial for being a Christian, would there be enough evidence to convict you?

Prayer cube

Roll the dice a few times and remember, you are praying for Togo in West Africa, and Canada today.

5 minutes

Stand on a chair

Finish today's cell by finding a chair (or wall in the garden) to stand tall on. Watch you don't stand on furniture you are not allowed to or make anything dirty!
Take it in turns to pray for boldness to be given to Christians in Togo, Canada and also your own home village, town or city!
Pray for each other this week!

5 minutes

Get together with your Wise Person and check out these Web sites.

Wycliffe Bible Translators   **www.wycliffe.org.uk**

Arab World Ministries   **www.awm.com**

7 History Makers need faith

YOU WILL NEED

scissors

postcards (or similar size paper)

Impossible paper tear

The challenge is to see if you can get your whole body through a piece of paper the size of a post card. The answer is in Appendix D (page 58). But don't look at it too soon! When you have given up, then find out how to do it and try it for yourselves.

10 minutes

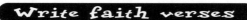

Write faith verses

Bless each other today in this worship section.

► Write a verse for each other in the cell.

► Write your verses in the same style as the famous chapter on 'History Makers' in the Bible. You'll find it in Hebrews 11.

► What is the word that keeps cropping up?

► Quietly work on your own and ask God to give you something for each person in your cell. Think about each person and what they could do with God.

► An example could look like this: 'By faith, Shane saw his best friend come with him to church!' or 'By faith, Catherine had courage and kept telling her best friends about God's love even when they laughed at her!'

► Now read them out to each other and encourage each other.

► Put up the word 'Faith' on the Worship Wall.

► Give each person their verses to take home.

5 minutes

Play a track

If you can, get hold of a copy of the album *Blitz* by thebandwithnoname. We suggest you play track 3, 'Amazing Grace'.

An alternative idea is for someone to bring to cell one of their favourite songs and introduce it, saying why they like it and what it teaches them about God.

4 minutes

• •

Be copycats of Jesus

Jesus is our model and example. We won't go far wrong if we copy him. Learn from Peter. Notice how he deals with people in the following two stories. Who did he learn this from?

Acts 9:32–43

Now try to find the similarities to the way Jesus was with people. Peter saw how Jesus helped people and it is amazing how similarly he did it.

Mark 2:1–12, Mark 5:35

In these stories who had the faith?

In Acts: Aeneas? Dorcas? Peter? Christians in Joppa?
In Mark: Jairus? Jesus? Daughter? Paralysed Man? His four friends? The Teachers of the Law?

Faith is present in these stories of God touching people. It might be that God wants to give you faith to see something happen. Faith is a gift of the Holy Spirit for a specific job. When praying for healing, it might be the person being prayed for who needs to have faith. In Acts 9, Aeneas had to take the first step when Peter commanded him to 'stand up!' In Dorcas' case she couldn't have had faith as she was dead, but Peter did.

The early church in Acts saw the church grow in dramatic ways.

Discuss

▶ Do we see the miraculous enough in our churches today?

▶ Have you ever seen God heal the sick? Have you ever prayed for the sick?

15 minutes

Elizabeth, aged 11, is from Paraguay

(can you feel the faith that this girl has?)

'My name is Elizabeth and I'm 11 years old. My family are Christians and until last year I went to a Christian school. Then we got too poor to be able to pay for the school, so my parents sent me to the state school. It's very different here, but I think it's God that sent me here. You see I've been asking around and I haven't been able to find anyone else who's a Christian. I've started praying for my friends and teachers. Actually, I'm praying for the whole school to come to know God. I've tried telling them about God, but it's hard to get people to listen. I prayed that God would send some other people to help me. That's when God sent the Tekove team. (Tekove is a King's Kids Schools Team in Paraguay. Tekove means 'Hope'.) They now come every few weeks and tell us about Jesus and how He can make a difference in our lives. After they've been everyone wants to talk about God. I'm glad He sent me here and I'm glad He answered my prayer.'

PARAGUAY

2 minutes

Meet thebandwithnoname:

thebandwithnoname is the touring band for an organisation called Innervation Trust. Innervation wants to set up a schools band in every major city in the UK. That is, a band that works exclusively in the secondary schools of a city doing assemblies, lessons and concerts and telling young people about Jesus. Our first team is already up and running in the schools of Liverpool and we are currently recruiting for teams in Cambridge and Colchester. thebandwithnoname's job is to tour around, the UK and beyond, telling everyone they can about the vision of Innervation and the schools teams.

Questions for the boys

The Big Cell – Were you all into music, God etc when you were young?

Chip K – Yeah, definitely. Our church used to do big musicals for special occasions and I was always involved when I was little in one way or another. And as far as being into God, well, I got saved when I was four and I've never rebelled since.

The Big Cell – What got you started in music, dance and doing this to spread the Good News?

Bobsta – I made a move from the mainstream to the Christian music industry through meeting our manager and producer several years ago. From a young age I knew God had given me a gift in music and dance but for many years I used it for myself and my own personal gain. I believe all artists have a responsiblity to use their talents and their gifts for the glory of God and that is what I seek to do.

The Big Cell – What's good fun about what you do and what is tough?

Presha – We all love performing and sharing what we believe, so to be able to put all my time into thebandwithnoname is great. Sometimes its hard spending a long time on the road away from family and friends.

5 minutes

Creative prayer idea

Mustard seeds

Jesus said all we needed was 'faith the size of a mustard seed!' Right now, go out into the garden or pavement outside wherever you are meeting. Be careful please!

Take it in turns to plant or throw your seeds to the wind. In the Bible one of the pictures for the Holy Spirit is that he is like the wind of God.

Pray for thebandwithnoname as God leads them to schools and cities etc.

Pray for other Christians in the Music business too, like Daniel Bedingfield or Athlete.

Pray for your favourite band or singer. What can you pray in faith for them?

YOU WILL NEED

packet of mustard seeds

5 minutes

Prayer cube

Roll the cube a few times and remember to use the ideas to pray for Paraguay.

5 minutes

Prayer ideas for thebandwithnoname

Please pray that God will provide enough money for Innervation Trust and thebandwithnoname to keep going in their work, so that loads of young people can hear about Jesus.

Pray for thebandwithnoname as they tour. Pray that God will keep them safe on all their travels, and that he will use them.

5 minutes

Cell challenge for this week
Be a secret seed agent

You could walk around your school or neighbourhood in twos or threes praying for the people there and scattering seeds as you go. Not big handfuls, just one or two seeds at a time. Pray prayers of faith.

> **'The more you give your faith away the more you get it!' – Michael Green**

Web sites to check out with your Wise Person

the bandwithnoname **www.thebandwithnoname.com**

Innervation Trust **www.innervation.org**

For next cell bring a thank-you prayer. Be ready to make a list of all the ways that God blesses you.

8 History Makers are sharing people

Seeds and share

- ▶ Discuss how the seed praying went during the week.

- ▶ Think of someone who you can send a chocolate bar to through the post. Wrap it and write their address on it clearly. Decide who will post it and make sure you get the correct stamp to put on it.

- ▶ Share out the rest of the food and enjoy eating it.

10 minutes

YOU WILL NEED

biscuits, chocolate, sweets to share

wrapping paper

padded envelope

stamps

YOU WILL NEED

bean bag or empty plastic bottle

Grab

One person needs to be the number caller for this game.
Organise everyone else in the cell into pairs. Give each pair a number.
Ask the pairs to stand opposite each other.
You ought to have two straight lines as shown in this diagram. These lines are the team you are part of.

Team A	**1**	**2**	**3**
		Object	
Team B	**1**	**2**	**3**

As long as everyone knows their number then you can start.
Place the object to be grabbed in the very middle.
Now the caller calls out a number and the pair with that number leave their places to try and grab the object.
The idea of the game is to grab the object without the other person tagging you before you get back to your place. If you are tagged then you lose a point! If you get back to your place without being touched then you win a point for your team (the line you are in).
Don't grab too hastily or you will keep losing the point!

10 minutes

Count your blessings

In Psalm 103:1–2 it says that we should not forget all the blessings God gives us. David the writer makes quite a list. Have a look.

▶ You should each make a list of all the valuable things, people, abilities, possessions etc. that you have in your life.

▶ Put these lists up on the Worship Wall. Each of you speak out a 'Thank you' prayer to the Lord.

▶ Remember to put up today's word which is 'Share'.

10 minutes

Put stuff in it's right place

As History Makers we need to get Jesus' perspective on all the stuff we have. Look at what God did with the first Christians.

Acts 4:32–35

Do you find sharing easy? What is hardest for you to share?
Are you rich? Compared to most in the world today all of us using this cell material are classed as rich. No doubt about it!

Read Matthew 19:16–24

Jesus speaks to a rich young man. Why did Jesus ask him to sell all his possessions? Is it wrong to be rich?
Look what choice the young man made!
Jesus himself talked about 'treasure in heaven' and 'treasure on earth'. Look it up in Matthew 6:19–21.
What does this mean? What's the difference between the two?

15 minutes

Bruna Garcia from Paraguay is 11 years old.

My mum has been praying for the children of Paraguay for years and years. For 3 years we've been going into the slums and teaching the children who don't go to school. We do a Bible club, teach them to read and do Maths and then we give them chocolate milk and a snack. Mum started to get a burden from God for the deaf children. Most of them don't go to school and it's difficult for them to be with hearing people because no-one thinks they are important. But to God they are very important, so we went to sign language classes in Brazil to learn how to tell them about God who loves them. Now we have a deaf boy in the group in the slums. I translate everything that the teacher is saying and help him make friends with the others. I also help him to learn so that one day he can go to school.

Now we're going to start a Tekove team in my city. My Mum is going to be the leader, but the rest of the team are just kids like me. We'll be going to 12 schools to share about Jesus. I go to school in the morning, so I'll be on the afternoon Tekove team. My cousin who goes to school in the afternoon will take my place in the morning team. We're going to have to be very careful to study hard in the rest of our time, but I think it's important for other kids to learn about God even if they don't have Christian parents to take them to church.

PARAGUAY

`2 minutes`

Cell group give away

If God asked you to, would you be willing to give away anything you owned? Look at the lists you made during Worship.
Ask God to speak to you about how he wants you to share (or even give away). After 2/3 minutes, ask the others what they thought God was saying to them. Keep asking God this week about it. If you feel God wants you to give something away, bring it to cell next time you meet.

Prayer cube

This week you are praying for South America, the continent that Bruna in the story comes from. Throw the prayer cube four times.

`13 minutes`

WISE PERSON

Talk to your Wise Person about what you should bring to the cell meeting to share or give away.

9 History Makers are alert at all times

If you keep to the suggested times of these activities you will be able to do both. If you prefer, you can choose to do just one of them.

Giants keys

YOU WILL NEED

a blindfold

a set of keys

▶ One person is blindfolded and led to the centre of the circle. Place a bunch of keys at their feet.

▶ The Welcome leader points silently to someone who has to creep as quietly as they can up to the keys, take them and return to their place.

▶ At this point the person in the middle has to guess who took them.

▶ A harder option is for the blindfolded person to point in the direction of a noise if they hear it. They catch the person out if they point right at them.

8 minutes

Wink murder

YOU WILL NEED

a piece of paper for each person, or a deck of cards

▶ Pass out the bits of paper or the cards and the one who gets the marked paper or the Joker is the 'murderer' for the game.

▶ The 'murderer' has to start to 'kill' people by winking at them, but the idea is for him or her not to get caught or be seen.

▶ When someone realises they were winked at they need to 'die' – but to keep the fun and tension in the game, die a few seconds after the wink. Enjoy being theatrical about it!

▶ After a while, people can 'challenge' by telling everybody who they think the murderer is. If they are right, the game starts again. If they are wrong, they have to die, and the game carries on.

▶ The game is over when everybody except the murderer is dead or the murderer is discovered.

▶ You may now give out the paper/cards again and repeat the game.

8 minutes

Last week you were asked to bring something you are prepared to give away for this week's cell.

The Worship leader for the cell today should choose a favourite praise song and explain why they have chosen it. God loves a cheerful giver, so a cheerful praise song would be appropriate for this time.

▶ During the song, each person should come and place their offering at the Worship Wall.

▶ At the end of the song, each person should pray a short prayer to the Lord, asking Him to bless someone else through their offering.

▶ The cell needs to decide who is going to receive these items. Check ideas with your Wise Person.

▶ Put up the words 'A job to be done' on the Worship Wall.

5 minutes

The Good News is for the whole world

Read the following

Matthew 24:12–14 and Acts 1:8

These verses say that one day the whole world will have an opportunity to hear the Gospel. This hasn't happened yet.

What do you think is stopping this from happening?

4 minutes

YOU WILL NEED

a photocopy of Appendix E for each cell member

a hidden copy of Appendix F – the answers

a pen or pencil

Where on earth is it?

▶ Using the the 'Where on earth is it?' activity sheet, you have 4 minutes to match the country names to their correct place on the map – all the countries you need have been shaded and numbered.

▶ Draw lines from the names to the nations.

▶ After your time is up, bring out the answers and see who got the most right.

7 minutes

work it out

The 11 nations in the activity you have just done are all in an area of the world some Christians call the '10/40 Window'. We all know what the equator is – an imaginary line around the middle of the Earth. The 10/40 Window is made of two more imaginary lines: one 10 degrees north of the equator and the other 40 degrees north of the equator.

So what's so special about this 'Window'?

Well, many nations in the 10/40 Window have heard very little about the good news of Jesus – many people have never heard of Him at all. These are the countries that have to be reached and told about Jesus before anyone can say the whole world has heard the Good News.

Did you notice when we read Matthew 24:12–14 that it said 'Then the end will come'? History will end and the world will see the return of Jesus. Christians call it 'the second coming'.
We're going to pray for these countries now.

Creative prayer idea

Pass the country

- ▶ Put the pieces of paper into your container.
- ▶ Sit in a circle and start to play a CD.
- ▶ You play this game like pass the parcel – when the music stops, pull out a piece of paper, read what it says and pray what it tells you for a couple of minutes until the music starts again.

15 minutes

YOU WILL NEED

a cut up copy of Appendix G

a container such as a hat, a bag or a box

WISE PERSON

Ask your Wise Person about who you could give the items from your offering to.

Web sites to check out with your Wise Person.

Barnabas Fund   **www.barnabasfund.org**

Christian Solidarity Worldwide email   **csw@csw.org.uk**

10 History Makers have a destiny!

A. Join the dots

Can you join the nine dots with 4 straight lines. Once you start you are not allowed to lift your pencil or pen from the paper.

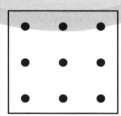

Answer in Appendix D (page 58).

4 minutes

YOU WILL NEED

five coins

B. Five coins

Put 5 coins out on the table like this.
You may only move one coin.
The idea is to create 4 coins in a row, but
without losing 3 in a row in the other direction.
Answer in Appendix D (page 58).

4 minutes

C. Above or below?

A		EF
	BCD	G

Where does 'H' for History Maker go? Above or below the line? Why?
Answer in Appendix D (page 58).

4 minutes

Pour out your hearts to Him

In Psalm 62:8 it says, 'Tell Him all your problems' or in some versions of the Bible, 'Pour out your hearts to Him', so we are going to do that today.

▶ Read the following verses from the Psalms. Someone should read them out, slowly and thoughtfully, while the others listen.

▶ At the same time, another person should pour water gently and quietly from a jug into a bowl.

▶ Everyone else can listen and watch. Let it be a sign of pouring your heart out to God, as you agree with the words from the Psalms in your heart.

Lord our Master, your name is the most wonderful name in all the earth!
It brings you praise in heaven above.
You have taught children and babies to sing praises to you. This is because of your enemies.
And so you silence your enemies and destroy those who try to take revenge.
Psalm 8:1 & 2

Praise the Lord, you angels. Praise the Lord's glory and power.
Praise the Lord for the glory of his name. Worship the Lord because he is holy.
The Lord's voice is heard over the sea.
The glorious God thunders.
The Lord thunders over the ocean.
The Lord's voice is powerful.
The Lord's voice is majestic.
The Lord's voice makes the lightning flash.
Psalm 29:1–4 & 7

A deer thirsts for a stream of water,
In the same way I thirst for you, God.
I thirst for the living God.
When can I go to meet him?
Day and night, my tears have been my food.
People are always saying,
'Where is your God?'
When I remember these things,
I speak with a broken heart.
Psalm 42:1–4

All stand and pray out loud together like one voice for 60 seconds (longer if you want to of course!). Forget others next to you and don't listen to them. Pour out your heart to the Lord. Tell Him you love Him. Tell Him what you think about Him.

Put the word 'Destiny' up on the Worship Wall.

10 minutes

Paul

Much of the New Testament was written by a man called Paul.
Read the story of how Paul, a young man in his early twenties, became a Christian.

Acts 9:1–19

Questions

What do you know about Paul before this happened to him?
Do you know what he did afterwards with his life?

Paul knew what his destiny was

Even though he experienced being arrested, locked up, beaten up, and shipwrecked in a storm at sea, he was still confident that God was looking after him.

Now Read the story for yourselves.

Acts 27:20–26

15 minutes

CONGO

Andy Kennedy's Story

Andy was born in Africa in a country called Congo. He is an identical twin and his twin brother Douglas was born first, just twenty minutes before Andy. The Doctor in charge was Andy's dad! When they were just days old, an African nurse came to visit. She saw the little baby boys and pointing to them said 'He (Douglas) will become a doctor when he is older and he (pointing now to Andy) will become a minister of the gospel'. Andy's mum and dad heard this but kept it to themselves until Andy and Douglas were much older, 30 to be precise. Amazingly, what the nurse had said had come true!

Cherith is 12 and lives in England. She was the first to start a Big Cell group with her friends and use this material. This story is included because it will be young people like Cherith who will see the UK changed.

Cell is brill because we get to figure out and learn stuff about Jesus in our own ways, which is easier to relate to. It's fun because we're not always listening to the adults, who get everything right the whole time. We have to figure things out for ourselves and we don't get bossed around! It's easier to relate to the Bible when we put it in our own everyday words and we get to study with our friends who we see all the time and who we're close to. It's good to have a Wise Person to explain things that are a bit too complicated for us to understand and so our faith can grow. Meeting together is really great, and we always make sure we have time to pray for each other so we can encourage one another. I'm praying God will speak to us as a group and encourage us to grow in our faith even when we're at school where everyone else seems to enjoy sin. CELL IS SOOOO GROOVY!'

5 minutes

Connecting into God's mission for you

Journal Time

Questions and ideas to talk about and write in your journals

▶ What age will you be in ten years time? What would you like to be doing with your life?

▶ Destiny isn't just about the future – it starts now. What interests and gifts had God given you and are you developing them?

▶ How well do you trust God, like Paul did, in difficult situations?

10 minutes

Prayer cube

Roll the cube a few times and pray for the UK this time.

5 minutes

Pray for each other

Stand in a circle and each of you pray for the person on your right. After one minute, change direction and start to pray for the person on your left. Ask God to bless them so that they will be a blessing to others.

2 minutes

Web sites to check out with your Wise Person

DC Talk and Jesus Freaks   **www.jesusfreaks.net**

King's Kids, a ministry of Youth With A Mission (YWAM)
www.kingskidsengland.co.uk

(King's Kids offers short-term missions experiences for 10–18 year olds and also the whole family. Under 10s must be accompanied by a parent or guardian.)

Appendix A

Instructions to make your Worship wall

1   This worship wall needs to be prepared in advance. It is easily transportable if made from cardboard. It can either lean against a wall, or if folded, it will free stand.

2   Decorate it in some way so it is attractive. We painted ours white with ready-mixed paint available from any art store. Allow the paint to dry and sponge-print 'bricks' using a large sponge, to imitate a brick wall pattern. You could either do red or brown bricks. When this is dry, we painted the words 'worship wall' along the bottom in a graffiti style. You could buy brick-patterned wallpaper or draw and paint any shapes you wish.

3   Photocopy the four 'W's: WELCOME, WORSHIP, WORD and WORK IT OUT

4   Each week attach them to the worship wall as you use them with blu tac. You could mount the four W's or laminate them if you wish.

welcome

49

I think... worms

proto worm

Work it out. Without it

Appendix B

Sorting out His-story

Puzzle

Sort out the story matching the parts of the story to the right chapter. You will need to photocopy the next 3 pages and cut out the pieces.

Chapter One

Chapter Two

Chapter Three

Chapter Four

Chapter Five

Chapter Six

Chapter Seven

Chapter Eight

Chapter Nine

Chapter Ten

For 2000 years, the followers of Jesus have been increasing on the Earth. Today there are well over a billion believers! However there are still lots of people to tell. About 1.2 billion people have never heard the Gospel!

Chapter Eleven

Chapter Twelve

Since the Cross, Satan has still been active on planet Earth; he is angry and afraid and knows his time is running out before he is finally judged and locked away. Satan knows that people who give their lives to Jesus and become children of God are no longer under his power.

Chapter Thirteen

So Jesus came to Earth and showed people what God was doing. He loved the poor and healed the sick, raised the dead and showed His power and authority. He told lots of stories, teaching people truth and how to become friends with God again.

But God had a plan to rescue the world He loved so much. He decided He would go himself, as the Son, and become a human being and rescue His creation. God knew only a perfect human being could beat Satan and win back the special friendship. To beat Death meant He himself would have to die!

Man and woman are tricked by Lucifer who uses a snake to get them to disobey God. Adam and Eve lose their special close friendship with God and come under the power and control of Satan, another name for Lucifer.

God creates human beings. It is quite a risk. They are not like robots with no ability to make choices. Will they choose to love God? At first God enjoys a wonderful friendship with Man!

God creates a beautiful world in an amazing expanding universe.

A terrible thing happens in Heaven. A beautiful angel called Lucifer is destroyed by his own pride and leads a rebellion against God. Lucifer and other angels are removed from the presence of God and thrown out of Heaven. Lucifer tries to get humans to join in the rebellion.

This terrible Fall from their special place as friends of God brings with it so much pain and suffering, evil and selfishness. This sin spreads like a disease throughout the world. The evil gripping the hearts of men and women breaks God's heart!

No one would be forced to accept this love of God in Jesus, or His rescue plan. It would be a choice – either accept Jesus, who is the truth and the life, and is the way back to Father God, or reject Him and be separated from Him forever!

When Jesus was killed, Satan thought he'd won. But it was Satan who had walked into God's trap! Jesus' death on the Cross is the most important event in all of history. When Jesus said the words 'It is finished!' he meant he'd completed the rescue mission. The resurrection is the final proof. Jesus beat death and destroyed Satan's power and the power of sin over human beings. He made a way to have special friendship with God again!

After the Resurrection, Jesus leaves his friends but says it is best that He does so because the Holy Spirit will be sent to live in them and help them! The Spirit is the sign of the special friendship having been won back.

Jesus is coming soon but first we must finish the rescue mission started by Jesus. It could be that we are in the final chapter of God's Story. It still needs to be written. It needs to be written BY YOU!

Solution

Chapter One

God creates a beautiful world in an amazing expanding universe.

Chapter Two

God creates human beings. It is quite a risk. They are not like robots with no ability to make choices. Will they choose to love God? At first God enjoys a wonderful friendship with Man!

Chapter Three

A terrible thing happens in Heaven. A beautiful angel called Lucifer is destroyed by his own pride and leads a rebellion against God. Lucifer and other angels are removed from the presence of God and thrown out of Heaven. Lucifer tries to get humans to join in the rebellion.

Chapter Four

Man and woman are tricked by Lucifer who uses a snake to get them to disobey God. Adam and Eve lose their special close friendship with God and come under the power and control of Satan, another name for Lucifer.

Chapter Five

This terrible Fall from their special place as friends of God brings with it so much pain and suffering, evil and selfishness. This sin spreads like a disease throughout the world. The evil gripping the hearts of men and women breaks God's heart!

Chapter Six

But God had a plan to rescue the world He loved so much. He decided He would go himself, as the Son, and become a human being and rescue His creation. God knew only a perfect human being could beat Satan and win back the special friendship. To beat Death meant He himself would have to die!

Chapter Seven

No one would be forced to accept this love of God in Jesus or His rescue plan. It would be a choice – either accept Jesus, who is the truth and the life, and is the way back to Father God, or reject Him and be separated from Him forever!

Chapter Eight

So Jesus came to Earth and showed people what God was doing. He loved the poor and healed the sick, raised the dead and showed His power and authority. He told lots of stories, teaching people truth and how to become friends with God again.

Chapter Nine

When Jesus was killed, Satan thought he'd won. But it was Satan who had walked into God's trap! Jesus' death on the Cross is the most important event in all of history. When Jesus said the words 'It is finished!' he meant he'd completed the rescue mission. The resurrection is the final proof. Jesus beat death and destroyed Satan's power and the power of sin over human beings. He made a way to have special friendship with God again!

Chapter Ten

Since the Cross Satan has still been active on planet Earth; he is angry and afraid and knows his time is running out before he is finally judged and locked away. Satan knows that people who give their lives to Jesus and become children of God are no longer under his power.

Chapter Eleven

After the Resurrection, Jesus leaves his friends but says it is best that He does so because the Holy Spirit will be sent to live in them and help them! The Spirit is the sign of the special friendship having been won back.

Chapter Twelve

For 2000 years, the followers of Jesus have been increasing on the Earth. Today there are well over a billion believers! However there are still lots of people to tell. About 1.2 billion people have never heard the Gospel!

Chapter Thirteen

Jesus is coming soon but first we must finish the rescue mission started by Jesus.
It could be that we are in the final chapter of God's Story. It still needs to be written. It needs to be written BY YOU!

Appendix C

Prayer Cube:

Cut out the shape below and glue together. Remember to fold in the flaps carefully and glue as well.

Pray and ask God to send more workers into the most un-reached places of the world.

Go and open doors and windows where you are meeting, asking God to open up opportunities for the Good News to be spread by His people.

Pray for the country mentioned in today's story. Ask God to raise up the children of that land to know Him.

Thank God for the Jesus film and how it has been used by Him all over the world. Ask Him to keep using it.

Pray for a friend at school by name

Pray for the Christians of the country in the story to have courage, boldness and unity to reach their nation.

Appendix D

Answers page

Session One
World mission quiz

b, c, b ,c, c, a

Session Five
Newspaper stand problem

Put the newspaper under a closed door with each person standing on each side of the closed door. Now you can't touch each other.

Session Seven
Impossible paper tear

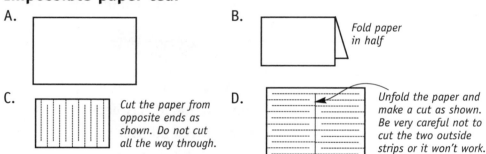

A.

B. Fold paper in half

C. Cut the paper from opposite ends as shown. Do not cut all the way through.

D. Unfold the paper and make a cut as shown. Be very careful not to cut the two outside strips or it won't work.

E. *You will now be able to open it up and it should be in a huge circle shape, big enough to climb through. The thinner the gaps between cuts, the bigger it gets!*

Session Ten
A. Join the dots

The only way to solve this is to draw out of the box. Starting on one of the corner dots, draw a straight line up one side and continue out of the box, then draw a diagonal line back through the box joining two dots, carrying on out of the box again. Draw a horizontal line back to the original starting place and then one final line diagonally to the opposite corner.

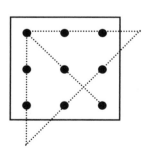

B. Five coins

Pick up one of the end coins and place it on top of the corner coin.

C. Above or below?

It goes on top of the line as the letters on the top are all made up of straight lines, while the letters under the line have curved edges.

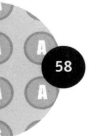

58

Appendix E

Where on earth is it?

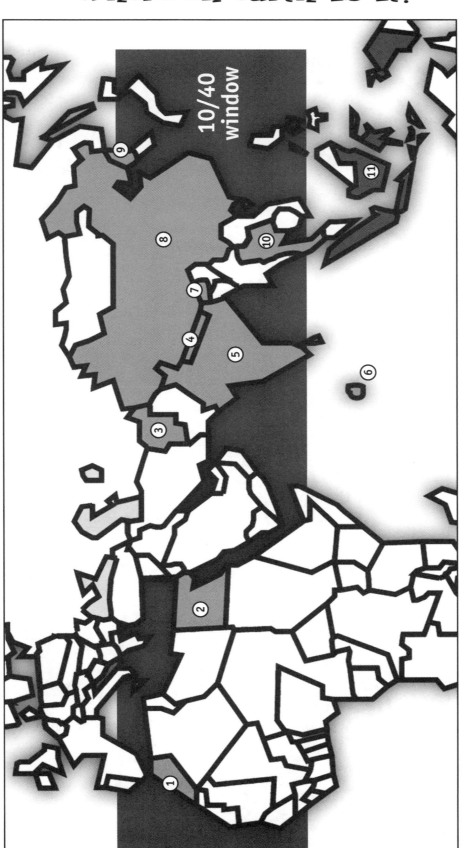

10/40 window

Indonesia

China

India

North Korea

Morocco

Afghanistan

Bhutan

Maldives

Thailand

Nepal

Egypt

Appendix F

Where on earth is it? (Answers)

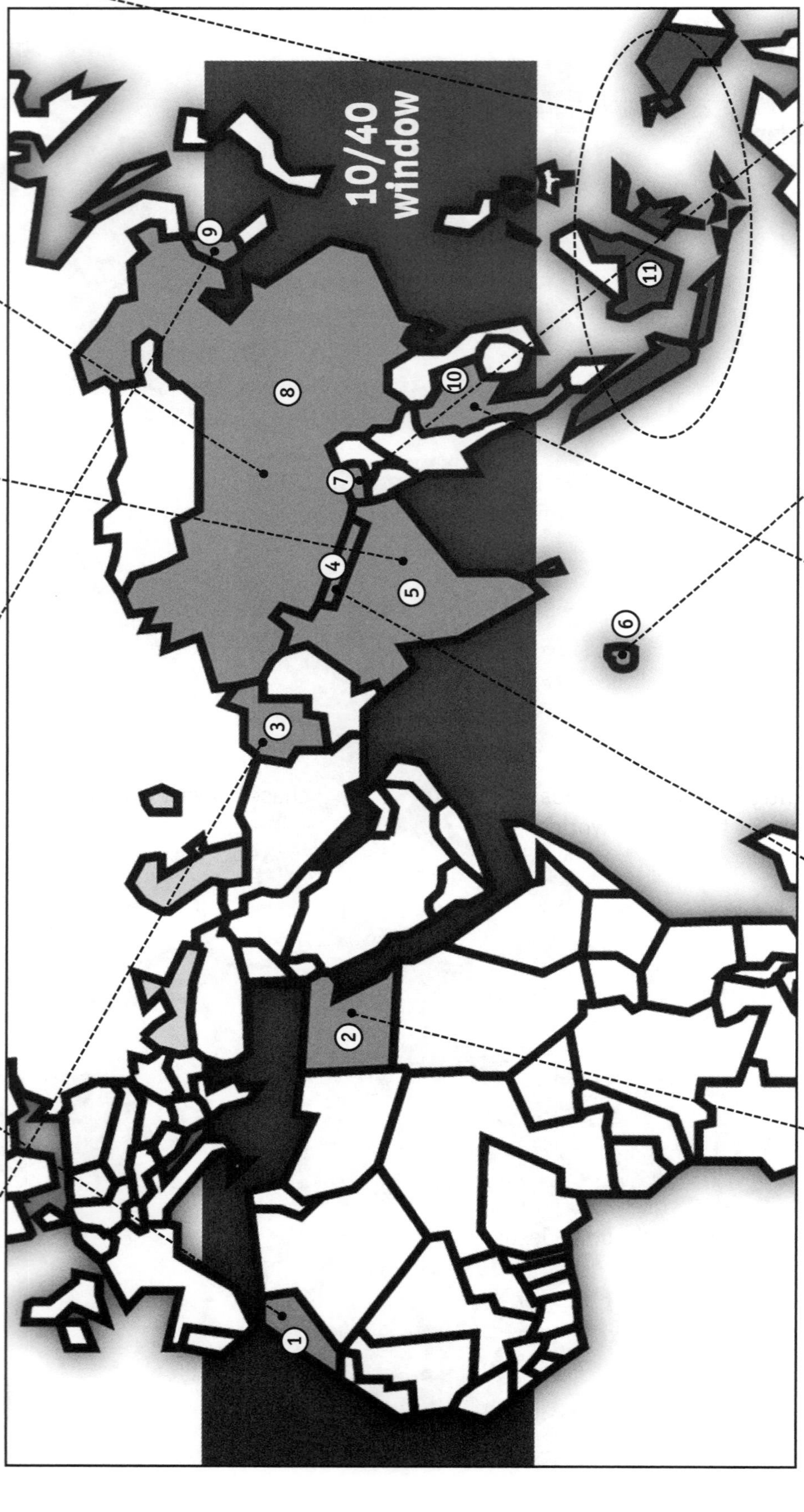

Indonesia
China
India
North Korea
Morocco
Afghanistan
Bhutan
Maldives
Thailand
Nepal
Egypt
10/40 window
1
2
3
4
5
6
7
8
9
10
11

Appendix G

Pass the country

Prayer pointers to be photocopied and cut out for your hat or box.

Afghanistan

This country is in a time of recovery after the fighting and bombing that went on there after September 11.

Put your fingers on the map over Afghanistan. Ask God to bring his healing touch to the hurt and wounded people in Afghanistan.

China

Christians are beaten and put into prison for talking about Jesus, but millions of people are coming to Him anyway.
Stand up and link arms in your circle.

Pray that God will keep the Chinese Christians strong and united as they face very hard times.

Bhutan

This country is one of the most closed to the gospel in the whole world.
Go and stand on one side of a door.

Pray that God will open doors in Bhutan for His good news to pour in. Then go through the door, asking Him to send people to share God's love.

Egypt

A mainly Muslim nation, although there are many Christians who are part of the oldest church in the world, the Coptic Church. There are still many more who have never ever heard about Jesus.

Go and stand around the TV and pray for SAT-7, a Christian satellite channel which broadcasts in Egypt every evening. Pray that people would see the truth through their TVs.

India

India is full of people! The largest group of people who have not yet heard the Christian message live there.

Lie on the floor together and pray that God would send more workers to join those already working with the millions of families and children who sleep on the streets all over India.

Indonesia

This group of islands is heavily under Islamic control, and Christians there have been persecuted much more over the last 10 years.

Place a blanket or jumper over the head of one of the group and put them in the middle. Ask God for His mercy to be shown to Indonesia and for the spiritual darkness and oppression to be chased away. Now take off the cover.

Maldives

These popular tourist islands are still very closed to the Christian faith; those suspected of being Christians are arrested. Islam is the only religion allowed.

Global warming threatens the islands through rising sea levels. Drink a glass of water each and pray for Maldivians to be thirsty for the water of life that only Jesus can bring.

Morocco

Another increasingly popular tourist destination, Morocco in North Africa is also an Islamic nation. Despite the fact that there is no freedom for anyone to leave Islam, there is growing interest in the Gospel.

Divide yourselves into pairs with one person in each pair closing their eyes. The other person leads the 'blind person' around the room without bumping into the other pairs. Swap over so everyone gets a turn. Now pray for God to lead Moroccans into His truth and to have the courage to seek after God.

Nepal

Nepal is in the famous Himalayan Mountains and has 8 of the 10 highest mountains in the world. It is also the world's only Hindu kingdom. People are free to choose their religion but it is illegal to try and convert anyone else. It is a very poor nation.

Find a piece of bread or a biscuit. Take a small piece each and then pray for the hungry to be fed both physically and spiritually.

North Korea

This country is Communist, but the people still die of starvation. 100,000 Christians are believed to be in very tough prison camps. North Korea is one of the hardest places to be a Christian today in the whole world.

Everyone curls up in a small shape somewhere in the room on their own. Close your eyes and be very still and quiet. Think about young people and children who love Jesus and are suffering in prison. Ask God to make His presence very real to them all.

Thailand

This strongly Buddhist nation is known as the 'Land of Smiles' because people are so polite and hospitable there. The Christian church there has hardly grown in the last 400 years. Many Thais do not have a Bible in their own language.

Put one of your Bibles into the middle of the circle. Ask God to bless the Bible Translators who still have 29 Thai languages to go.

Useful Resources

Inflatable Globe (OPW3) STL £4.99

CD's/Cassettes

Children of the Cross Jim Bailey

Woopah Wahey Doug Horley

52 Scripture Songs Ishmael

A Gift from the Father H_2O

Where Angels Fear to Tread Matt Redman

Deeper Delirious

Blitz bandwithnoname

Here I am to Worship Tim Hughes

Books for Kids:

International Children's Bible New Century Version
(1991 Authentic Bibles)

Window on the World: When we pray God works
Daphne Spraggett with Jill Johnstone (2001 Paternoster)

Excellent full colour book with fun creative prayer ideas for various people groups! Cell could invent their own prayer topics using this resource. (there are also CDs of music and prayer that can accompany this book)

Jesus Freaks Dc Talk and the voice of the Martyrs
(2000 Eagle Publishing)

Books for Wise Persons:

Operation World: When we pray God works
Patrick Johnstone/Jason Mandryk (2001 Paternoster)

A remarkable book! Lots of background in stats and theology!

Eternity in the Hearts
Don Richardson (1981 Regal Books/Gospel Light USA)

Some inspiring stories of God reaching the unreached!